THE INSOMNIA POEMS

Grace Nichols was born in Guyana, and has lived in Britain since 1977. Her first collection, *I is a Long Memoried Woman* (1983) won the Commonwealth Poetry Prize. This was followed by four collections with Virago, *The Fat Black Woman's Poems* (1984), *Lazy Thoughts of a Lazy Woman* (1989), *Sunris* (1996), winner of the Guyana Prize, and *Startling the Flying Fish* (2006), poems which tell the story of the Caribbean, along with several poetry books for younger readers, including *Come on into My Tropical Garden* (1988), *Give Yourself a Hug* (1994), *Everybody Got a Gift* (2005) and *Cosmic Disco* (2013). Her three most recent poetry books are published by Bloodaxe: *Picasso, I Want My Face Back* (2009), *I Have Crossed an Ocean: Selected Poems* (2010) and *The Insomnia Poems* (2017). She was poet-in-residence at the Tate Gallery, London in 1999-2000 and received a Cholmondeley Award for her work in 2001. She lives in Sussex with the poet John Agard and their family.

GRACE NICHOLS

The Insomnia Poems

BLOODAXE BOOKS

ISBN: 978 1 78037 339 3

First published 2017 by
Bloodaxe Books Ltd,
Eastburn,
South Park,
Hexham,
Northumberland NE46 1BS.

www.bloodaxebooks.com
For further information about Bloodaxe titles
please visit our website or write to
the above address for a catalogue.

Supported using public funding by

**ARTS COUNCIL
ENGLAND**

BRENT LIBRARIES

BR
WEM

Cover design: Neil Astley & Pamela Robertson-Pearce.

Printed in Great Britain by Bell & Bain Limited, Glasgow, Scotland, on
acid-free paper sourced from mills with FSC chain of custody certification.

CONTENTS

For John
and for my sisters and brother,
Avril, Valerie and Dennis,
who all know that insomnia-feeling

Pray for the wakeful house,
friend, and the lit window

MARINA TSVETAEVA,
(tr. Elaine Feinstein)

Once Again

Once again
the hallway mirror
is startled by my 3am face –
a passing moon
across the stillness
of its lake –

The hallway mirror
that has regained
its silvered composure
but fuming within
the depths –
that it must always reflect.

One Night Comes Like a Blessing

Like a cruel lover or spiteful mistress
No-Sleep demands my restless attentiveness.

No-Sleep prefers me stripped –
a dark projectionist

winding and unwinding the reel of my thoughts.
An old grained movie I can't switch off –

a starring of loves and loss, TV footage,
soft tears, mortifications, smothered laughs.

Then, one night comes like a blessing.
A visitation of wings that sees me falling.

Whoever wants me now, I am swimming
towards my House of Dreams.

Let no one disturb this peace.
Let no one shake me

even from the branches of nightmares.
Come morning I am reborn again –

a fresh-faced Eve – emerging from the rib's shadow –
ready to meet the daily pandemonium of living.

The Projectionist

Even the projectionist
has abandoned his reeling tonight –
camera-eye switched off –

      No flickering images
              shifting like fishes
No changing thoughts
              reflecting
the constant breaking
      and remaking of the world

He too is laid low by the never
ending streams of sorrow
that leave their shadow below the heart.

Tonight the projectionist offers no new footage.
Just a blank screen in the dark –
a silent homage to the sorry of the world.

A Brief Odyssey

The toddler whose body was laughter
happy even after they had to flee
the grey rubble of what was once home.

A live wire, all jumps and chants,
he repeated the words of his father;
Eu-rope, boat-trip, new-home-new-home.

Dressed as if for an outing, a great adventure,
he, his brother and anxious parents,
all headed for the Aegean – Homer's mythic sea –

But the night it was dark
and the sea it was uncalm
and the boat – an overcrowded dinghy
set sail like a gamble against an hourglass.

Ill wind, ill-fated odyssey,
leaving only a father to tell
the dazed tale of how they all slipped
his clinging fingers turned to sand –

The live wire, all jumps and chants,
returned by the abiding manes of the sea...
a small and casual sacrifice
on the shore of Poseidon's omnivorous heart.

Moon-mothers

Sometimes, being a mother
is much like being the moon.

You wax, you wane,
you watch, you half-bloom.
You cast a silver net from the navel
where the bloodling once swooned.

You grow gibbous with worry –
all the phases of being lunar –
Awaiting the flooding footsteps
of a returning son or daughter.

And when at long last you hear that key
turning in the night's uncertain light
(as pearl is to oyster)
how you begin to shimmer.

Suddenly life becomes a boon –
Once more you melon into full moon.

The Accomplice

The dream that is not interpreted is like a letter that is not read

RABBI CHISDA, *The Talmud*

Swan on left   Snake on right
swimming unswervingly
towards each other.
Two archetypes

Head-on-course
for the re-enactment
of some piece
of primeval river-drama.

Closer and closer –

Already Snake rears
his head to strike.
I fear for the grace
of Swan's life.

But calm and unruffled
as if removing an obstacle
she opens her beak wide –
Swallows all of him whole –

His foiled-coil emphasising even more
the downy crescent of her throat.
Too heavy to fly
and yet she manages –

Her gorged-mission accomplished,
circling me like an accomplice.

An Insomniac's Attempt at Her Own Self-hypnosis

Ignore the faceless thoughts
pressed like sunflowers
looking askance at an entrance
as if your brain was a greenhouse
or a glass case of bargains at Harrods.

Give your worries to the wind
feel your limbs growing limp
feel the ancient weight of night
upon your eyelids –

Forget the world-problems you cannot fix
the mounting to-do list
the appointment you forgot
to keep with your own hypnotist.
you're beginning to drift –

Be a midnight optimist.

Another Day

Eventually,
I get up to read –

the milk of morning
spilling across the page.
Another day sets sail.

At the Edge of the Table

(with apologies to Brazilian poet, Carlos Drummond de Andrade)

At the edge of the table there is a hand.
There is a hand
at the edge of the table.

At the edge of the table there is a hand.
I will never forget this observation
in the life of my tired eyes.

Just as you, Carlos, will never forget
that there was a stone in the middle
of the road –

I will never forget that at the edge
of the table, there is a hand – my hand.

Nightmare

Perhaps I was dreaming
Perhaps I was between sleep and wake
Perhaps I should have dialled 999

When in a city, I don't now remember –
Could have been Leeds, Birmingham, Leicester –
I awoke, or dreamt I awoke in the early hours
to the slamming of a car door,
raised voices, a man and a woman arguing.
(What's so bad about that?)
All over the world men and women are arguing.

I imagined they were lovers
I imagined their nearby house
I imagine her going inside
I imagine her shutting him out

I imagine him angry
His voice sounded deadly
Open the effing door
or I'll have me shoes in your blood

Perhaps I was dreaming
Perhaps I was between sleep and wake
Perhaps she opened the door.

Wherever They Lie

As water bathing stones –
play softly over the bones
of daughters, gone to the violent storms
of those who should be their brothers.
When the night rains blow, hear them whisper;

Do not forget our deaths.
Do not sweep us as crimes
of passion under the carpet
but commemorate us –
even as the unknown soldier
at the cenotaph of your hearts.

May the eternal mother
seek them out wherever they lie –
May she cup each soul in her hands' home
before setting them upwards
like butterflies from a tear-soaked earth.

Night–coos

In the absence of sleep
I listen to the house
as it breathes

      *

In the absence of sleep
I simply keep
Night, company

      *

In the absence of sleep
I see the metal fishes
of falling bombs

      *

Teach me again, Night,
your latent lullaby
that slept me as a child

Insemination of Pig Between Sleep and Wake

It isn't as if I demanded to dine
on a trough of pearls or insisted
on a pig-husband all to myself.

In the tough old world of Pig Husbandry,
I accepted the score –
twenty females to a boar. In any case

It implied I was the indispensable-spawner.
No I don't ask too much of life –
just my swill and my litter of little trotters;

And of course a real boar –
a real flesh and blood swine –
to straddle me in pigsome affirmation.

Now I can hardly bear to meet
the rutting eyes of my sidelined-hubby –
his unaccepting-acceptance

as he watches me burningly –
his work usurped. His musky-essence guided
by platonic fingers of profit into my essential bits.

O my bristle-bodied grunter. Is this cold new intimacy
all we get from man? We who die a million
squealing deaths to save his bacon.

Learning

Neither my lavender-scented pillow
nor the crescent beaches of my eyelids
will take me tonight into sleep.
Not like she who slept her azure-lidded
in Keats' 'Eve of St Agnes'.

I will try the usual childish tricks
of counting sheep, then lambs, then stones.
I'll practise breathing like the sea.
I'll turn towards the planets.
Nothing will work.

Well, I've decided to stop trying.
Across the open memory of ocean
I am learning to make
No-sleep into a Life-buoy –
a floating friend I can drift with...drift...

Sleeping Beauty

They never mentioned the curse
of the thirteenth fairy or the mitigating wish
of the twelfth who hadn't yet spoken.
Or how they'd burnt every spindle in the land.
Instead my royal father and mother
watched over me like velveted falconers –

Every breath I take
Every move I make
(haven't I heard that sung somewhere?)

Yet in my fifteenth year, fate construed
to let their eyes mislay me for a moment
and like a fallen shawl unnoticed by its owner,
I slipped to the tower where my destiny
(in the shape of an old woman as spindly
as her spindle) sat waiting to deal me.

You know the rest, how I begged a try.
Pricked as predicted, I fell out of time,
my contagion sweeping the whole palace into sleep –
the king, the queen, the maids, the cooks,
the scullery boy, the horses, the dogs,
down to the flies on the wall; the doves on the roof.

I hibernated for a hundred years.
Wars raged, inflation flourished,
but I slept on, nourished
on the black milk of sleep,
I became a legend, a ravishing rose
in an impenetrable forest of thorns.

You can imagine how waking up –
even to a prince's kiss, was for me,
a traumatic second birth.
What if I said that I preferred
my enchanted dark
to the active daylight of the world.

Memory is its own vision

GEOFFREY HILL

The Brain – is wider than the Sky –
For – put them side by side –
The one the other will contain
With ease – and You – beside –

EMILY DICKINSON

Night Muse

You who always come flooding back
in the shades of your original form –
but shot through now
with street lights and neon –
a glitzy black mother of pearl

Dressed in black olive
                            and onyx
drinking dark chocolate
                            and licorice
at the trendy Café Noir.

You who can reverse yourself
and light is born.

But I remember when you
were simply a dark astonishment
that allowed fireflies and stars to glow
as I star-gazed with my brother
at childhood's window

And you yourself bent down low
to harbour us in your arms.

Watershed

I only had to take a running dive
to feel her covering me.
She who hid me from the pursuing ones
(Sleep's nameless phantoms).

Wherever she was, was safety –
My H_2O mother.
Ocean, river, canal, sea.

How I swam through her fluidity –
The plasma of her gulf streams
the coral corridors of her bones.

But in a watershed moment
she delivered me
from my elementary world
back to dry shore.

Time to sink or swim
in my own river.
Time to be the fish
of my own ebb and flow.

Tonight My Childhood

Tonight my childhood sits
behind the shutters of my eyelids
bringing out one by one
my storehouse of treasures.
Tempting me back.

First the miracle fish;
one of the chosen
fallen out of the skies –
still pulsing wet
before my eyes

Next a half-ripe mango
wearing just enough
of the sun's halo.
The way I like it – a tarty
Buxton-spice sweetness

Then the flower
closest to my blood
blooming redly
into its own love-cup –
my ubiquitous hibiscus.

Tonight my childhood
delves deep into the small days
of my compulsive collections –
The freckled jewel of a telltale egg –
the one still missing

from the courida tree
I'd managed to climb,
my lucky black tamarind seed,
that old red-winking morning star –
Each an heirloom on her palm.

The Shadow-stealers

(remembering Edmay's words)

In the in-between hour
when shadows fall,
I race myself home
along the red-brick road
remembering Edmay's warning words:
'Wicked spirits can steal yuh shadow
while you grow sick they grow strong.'

In the deepening dusk
with the disappearing sun
and the jumbies
lurking round the bush,
I run, holding onto the shield
of my shadow – the shape I make
to take me through this world.

Diablesse

(The 'devil woman' of Caribbean folklore,
personified as a beautiful creole woman dressed in
the old-time finery of the costume of the islands.
She is said to prey particularly on young men who
often fail to notice her one goat-foot.)

All day long she's inside,
coolly preparing for the prospects of night,
prettifying her face and nails
mending the wear and tear
of her long frilly dress
which much always fall like a blessing
above the fault of her instep.

By nightfall she's ready as rain
unstoppable as a hurricane
emerging sultrily to that place
where instinct leads to find her prey.

Hours of suck-teeth waiting.
Hours of hoof-tapping pacing.
At last her impatience is rewarded
in the shape of some foolhardy
some young blood wending
his way from latenight party
with only a sleeping upstairs God
and firefly for company.

But has he taken any precaution
as preached by his womenfolk
against this eventuality?
No. Not even the most basic,
such as wearing his shirt inside-out.

So she jolts him with the tight bodice
of her breasts playfully running
a finger along the curve of his bicep,
her unmistakable scent matching perfectly
the patent warning inside his head,
even as he follows her in –
deeper and deeper into her busy ambushing.

As expected, he's never quite himself again.
Stamped with her insignia, he sits around
scribbling and daydreaming –
smiling foolish at the furious women in his life –
the we-told-you-so grandmother, mother, wife –
whispering in their oystered-ears
that one word, that one word... 'Diablesse'

As if like Saul at Damascus he'd been blessed –
this revelation into their mythic secret.

Our Pied Piper

The one we loved to death.
The family friend who visited every day

And sometimes even tucked us into bed
acting the voices of every story he read;

Entering our children-games with relish
wearing the daisy chains we made for his wrists.

The creeping magic of his white mice
(peeping familiar from his sleeves and pockets)

Should have given us a clue –
Instead I lived enchanted on his lap

And shoulders, reaching for the gifts
he hid like Easter eggs.

My answer when he said that he'd go blind,
was a tearful: *I will lead you never mind.*

He who nestled his true colours under
the golden branch of my parents' friendship –

Playing on the pliancy of our childhood
(our ring-of-hands, our gibberish-chants)

With the adept fingers of his music.
But on the cusp of puberty –

Holding fast my girlhood's newfound sustenance –
I had the strength to take back myself

From the one who felt I would follow him
through the door within the mountain.

Moon-calf

Because she runs with what she's been given
and remains an enigma –
Because the tides obey her.

Because she's our closest cosmic-neighbour.
Because she's woven a garment for herself
from the loom of sun's eternal summer.

Because she's my old biological calendar –
both shape-shifter and shadow-maker
(her trick of mind, her turn of eye)

Because she's our truest poet of the sky
I will state it, even at the risk
of being regarded as a moon-calf –

> for better or worse
> for richer or poorer
> awake or sleeper

I Love the Moon

Rain Rain

Not the thunderous
tropical downpour
making rushing rivers

And puddles
striving to turn
into big-woman ocean

But the steady
monotonous rhythm
of rain rain

Bringing the first
clear flavour
of boredom to my palette –

Whereas before
I was one
with the naked rain

Suddenly I was dressed
in the clothes
of my new separateness –

Sensing with a distinct sadness
that my country
called *Childhood* was over.

Happy are they who dream by night
and recall their dreams by day, O Lord,
for they shall rejoice

DANIELO KIŠ
(*The Legend of the Sleepers*,
tr. Michael Henry Heim)

Beyond the Dreaming Dark

Who was it –
that came to play last night
on the harp of my heart?

A bliss beyond the dreaming dark
a symphony of empathy
more beautiful than Mozart.

Sweeter than the tender grace
that made Caliban weep to dream again.

Streams of Mercy

(in memory of my younger sister, Claire)

If I had a recipe I would have given you, Claire.
Instead, we willed you on with prayers,
poultices, massages, but could only bear
witness to your body's failing ship –
your signals of distress.

Yet when I bent to embrace you
with my leaving kisses
my wreathing tears –
the frail sail of your arm lifted
to wrap me in a great compassion –

You who never wanted to leave
your own country for another –
neither New York nor Alabama.

May streams of mercy hymn you, my sister.
May heaven prove a haven and a harbour.
If I had a recipe I would have given you, Claire –

Easy as a leaf falling
Sudden as a shower of cleansing rain.

Snowdrops at the Hurst

Walking on the woodlands of the Hurst
surrounded by Shropshire's secluding hills,
I see you – a coverlet of white across the grass,

First flowers to brave a still wintry earth,
I bend to look closer
to observe your tiny cupolas –

Eve's frozen tears that shouldn't
be picked (according to lore)
and brought indoors.

Stay where you are,
fair maids of February –
Adorn the timeless green of earth.

Inside the warmth of the Hurst
young poets click their fingers
high on the bloom of words.

Rip Van Winkle

Well, I was homing it late,
after walking my dog in the hills,
when I met a strange band of men
who invited me to their game of nine pins –

I gladly accepted, drank fully of their flagons
and listened to their reveries as if they were friends.
As the game resounded in the hills,
little by little, I fell into a deep sleeping –

You know the rest.
When I woke up – my dog was gone,
my gun rusted, my beard
some ten fold long.

Bewildered, I hurried me down to the village,
where everyone stared at me like a phantom.
'Does nobody here know Rip Van Winkle?' I cried.
'Rip Van Winkle's over yonder,' they replied.

I looked and saw my younger double.
Rip Van Winkle (junior) now fully grown.
He challenged my identity and looked at me cold.
Only my elder daughter distilled a father's welcome.

Christ, I had misplaced twenty years of my life!
Sleep had taken both my companions and wife.
I'd much rather have her back, *Her-Indoors*,
so adept at finding me husbandly-chores.

Now I, Rip Van Winkle, wander still –
a lonely moon among the hills –
From within the resounding valleys,
a euthanasia-ing breeze whispers: *Sleep, Rip, sleep.*

Gift from a dead father

Only the nimble·hands
of a dream could have created it –

The subtle blend of leaves like flowers
the fruit-like presence
of its lyrical colours –

my undemonstrative father
with his demonstrative late gift –
like a stored love made visible
bringing, even now, a smile to my lips.

Parallel World

After you've woken up,
what you most remember
of your parallel world

is the drama of the talking fish
in search of its missing head – floating
about somewhere like the Cheshire cat's grin

the grown-up child-bride stepping forth
in her unbelievably tall shoes –
inbuilt with her own trousseau of food.

And arousing an ambivalence, the queen-bee
in the spider's web. Who knows whether
she's usurping predator or trapped victim?

On the verge of waking
your clubbing late-night daughter
has shrunk into a miniature –

A small Alice standing safely
on the palm of your hand.

The Myoclonic Jerk

That jolt that sometimes startles you
out of the brink of sleep –
That mini muscular seizure
as if you were falling into the deep!

Well, there's a name for it.
Wait for it – the *myoclonic* jerk –
Not to be confused with the twerk,
the backside's cheeky jiggling quirk –

No, the *myoclonic jerk*, may well be
(according to Carl Sagan, science-expert),
a throwback to the days when
our pre-human ancestors slept in trees.

To ensure they were in a secure position
for sleeping among the precarious branches
and leaves – the *myoclonic jerk* evolved –
making it seem as if you were falling
(in case you actually fell)
so you could adjust yourself. Well Well!

O my arboreal ancestors, thank you
for giving us the *myoclonic jerk* –
this behavioural-fossil still lurking
in our reptilian like a perk –
Still saving me from falling
a million years on.

Close to the Edge

All I remember after I'd woken up
is how we'd stood there
on the moon's dark edge
her curving side –
free from the rules of gravity
and how we were given an insight
into the sheer terror of infinite beauty
and how we caught the tail end
of a solar wind and got an inkling
of our own earthly weather system
as we clung to the sailing moon
through the turbulent tides of sleep
knowing we were close to the edge – in at the deep.

Dream Libation

Why do they all keep schtum –
the dead ones who visit me in dreams?
Both friends and relatives,
all silent witnesses –

Deities with considerate smiles
as if possessed of some
hidden knowledge,
I too will come to know – in good time.

Even the tall ancestral-looking figure
(encountered along my dream-way),
says not a word. Merely nods
his head for a shot of rum

from the unopened bottle
clutched in my hand like a talisman –
A timely reminder that
the spirits also like their spirits

Within the Gospels

Again and again your name
casts an asking-shadow within the gospels –

the fallen, saved from a stoning?
the possessed, saved from seven demons?

the penitent, washing those feet with your tears –
the one braving the bloodthirsty mobs to Calvary.

the one kneeling at the foot of the crucifixion
first witness to the resurrection.

Undenying and steadfast Mary –
Are you one and the same?

I am Mary Miriam of Magdalene.
I am the stigma-ta they can't erase.

To the Virgin of Guadalupe

With a kind but grave countenance
you observe, the lit candles,
the prayers rising like incense
for safe passage to new horizons –

They who set off with inadequate water
across parched deserts

They who enter sealed lorries
against their better judgement

Or hitch themselves to an inflatable star
against the mighty sea –

Reweaver-of-the-unravelled
Calm-centre-of-the-storm
Patroness of those driven
by direful necessity –

Consider them when
the only homecoming –
is a mirage.

When the only hope
within the drowning waves
is the resonance of your name.

Gilgamesh

For in the days that followed Enkidu's death –
Enkidu, my beloved companion,
I Gilgamesh, though sick with grief, rose up –
for I felt Death's shadow upon myself.

My journey took me to the mouth-of-all-rivers
to meet Utnapishtim (the Sumerian Noah
saved from the flood), an everyday man
who had found eternal life for himself
in the garden of the Gods.
There, I enquired how I, Gilgamesh,
already two-thirds divine may claim the third.

The task he set me seemed straight.
(No challenge, compared to the battle,
when with Enkidu, we sealed the fate
of the shape-shifting Humbaba.)
To gain entry into eternal-life, I must simply
stay awake for six days and seven nights.

Thus I laid down, resolving to beat the worm's dominion.
But immediately Sleep began to dance
like foggy sheep before me, outstaring my eyes.
Soon, Utnapishtim was shaking me awake.
I had failed big time –
and he had bread to prove it (the cunning bastard).

'Mark well, these seven loaves,' he intoned,
'baked each morning by my wife's own hands
while you were fast sleeping.
The first, now seven days old, is hard as a stone;
The second is leathery; the third soggy;
the fourth spotted with mould;
the fifth mildewed, the sixth beginning to stale.

47

While the fresh-baked seventh,
if you feel it, still carries the heat of the oven.'

So, it was that, I Gilgamesh,
whose name would become epic –
I Gilgamesh, King of Uruk,
Lord of the four-quarters
etcetera etcetera...
was denied a place at the Immortal table
and came to accept my death.

I who had slain the great Bull of Heaven
but could not defeat the silent lamb of sleep.

I was asleep but my heart stayed awake

SONG OF SONGS: *The Shulammite*

My Best Cure *(for John)*
(a guest house in Yorkshire)

In this strange guest house
where sleep won't come,
I toss, I turn,

the curtains lifting in the old
unsilvering mirror – the moors beyond –
a drift of hostile spirits.

So tonight I'll leave a light
against the ghosting dark
and rest my thoughts on you –

Ever welcoming of my
foreday-morning touch –
the one that awakens you –

My best cure for insomnia –
taking me once more to sweet inertia.

The Long Haul

(for John – early days)

Walking with you
on the Essequibo coast
in the dark –

A night full
of the bright fruits of stars
and the sound of the Who-You birds –

The river slapping
its heavy silk
against the green-heart wharf.

And later,
you caught in the net
of a well-deserved sleep,

As I come back
from my small death
to gaze into the enormity of life –

The flickering candlefly.
Sensing that
my flitting-days were over.

That with you who carry
the scent of the earth
in the sky of your armpit –

It would be
the long haul
towards the stars.

In the Meditating Dark

In the meditating dark
your body is a sand dune –
lightly I trace its form

In the meditating dark
an oasis blooms –
below the desert stars

Starry Night

For my part I know nothing with any certainty,
but the sight of the stars makes me dream

VINCENT VAN GOGH

Against the framing dark
        come the mystic orbs
of your haloed-stars

Sunflower-stars
        swept in the arms
in Night's cosmic dance –

Swirling whirls
        of peacock blues
and twilight hues

Night must have
        opened the vaults of her
milky mysteries to you –

Night must have
        carried you in the vortices
of her music –

So you could
        brushstroke her
with your starry gift.

Adam to Eve

(for Stanley Greaves and his Morning Mangoes painting)

I remember how your hands shook
as you handed me the dripping fruit
and how in one fell swoop
even as I savoured the forbidden juice
the caul of paradise vanished from our eyes
and we were transported by an inner glow
a sunripe alchemy from head to toe –

For it was the mango, my love,
that tempted you to bite its blush.
Manifera Indica, that first stirred –
the branches of our blood
the greed of your mouth.

Now in dreams we stand
in Eden's memorable river,
exchanging, under a transgressing moon,
the ambrosia of morning mangoes.

Forgive us O Apple for switching
the myth of your fallen bliss.

Baby Sleep

(Kalera at three months)

What dreams lie behind the soft shells
of your eyelids? What adventures
in the world you inhabit?

From the smile playing havoc with your lips
the half-opened flowers of your fists –
I would say you were in your bliss.

Perhaps, trying to walk before you can creep
on some sunny shore or basking once more
in the frog-leaps of your foetal existence.

Whatever you're doing, I'm the one awaiting,
the black pearls of your awakening.

Dawn Speaks of Dawn

When Night sleeping at his deepest
sleeping at his darkness, little by little,
I begin to unravel myself –

Stretching and spreading
in my fore-day morning dress –
The same old silver-grey one
I wearing from time immemorial yes.

Yet in it everyone adore me so
as soon as cock see me
he prick up and start to crow
and every piece of river, bush
and stone, acting new and shy

Like they just spring-up overnight
to bask in my firstlight.

Twin Sisters

The closeness of Dusk and Dawn –
When Dawn switch places with Dusk,
Night instead of day, is born.
When Dusk transfers herself as Dawn,
Sun is none the wiser to her form.

Waking-up London

Waking-up London opens itself
to the opening of shop fronts
          pigeons gusting
from the pavements being swept
like the drifting lift of coffee incense.

Opens itself to the offerings
of cathedrals –
          the cool resonance
of themselves.
O the bells of St Clements –

Opens itself to the waves
of early-bird commuters
          pressed (for now)
into the working-mould
of one beating humanity.

Meanwhile, the metal gods
of the building sites,
          cuds full of concrete blocks,
prepare to shoulder
the rising strain of glass and steel –

The syllables of many tongues
address the waking-up city.

Reflecting on Pebble

(after a painting by Lewes artist, Tom Walker)

How did it happen
the voice of pebble
shuffled and stroked
for millennia by sea
and the grey hands of wind?

An ordinary stone
rewarded for its patience
with the slow piercing of its throat –
One of the chosen from
millions of rolling stones.

And under Tom's hands
his coaching of Pebble –
Pebble began to bloom
Pebble began to sing
rising to the X-factor
of its cosmic beginnings.

In Search of Sleep

(after George Herbert's 'Peace')

Not Herbert's quest for peace
which began in a secret cave,
but simple sleep is all I crave.
So I took my insomnia down to the sea
where I watched each breaking wave –
but Sleep eluded me.

So I took myself to the dreaming forest
to see if that was where Sleep rested
but all I saw were lurking shadows
and leaves casting a mysterious glow;
Yes even among the rustling trees,
Sleep once again eluded.

So I went from the earthly
to the high heavenly planets
wondering if by any chance,
Sleep slept within their cosmic dance.
I watched them swirl but Sleep was nowhere –
only the endless music of the spheres.

On my early way home, whom should I meet?
But a dark figure robed to the feet.
'You'll not find, Sleep here,' he declared.
Not in sea, forest or swirling sphere.
For the one called Sleep is a crafty thief
who loves you most when you court him least.

Yet this nightly thief is guilty of no crime,
all he steals is your restless time –
your restless time which he repays tenfold –
for the ore of Sleep is more priceless than gold.'
So I took my insomnia home to bed
and there was wisdom in what the robed-one said.

Guitar

In the light and in the dark –
the guitar of the heart
keeps up its strumming
in a humming universe

The One You Don't See Coming

How I wish he would visit me more often;
The-One-You-Don't-See-Coming.
How I wish he would drink my limbs.

Many a night I've tried to seduce him –
herbal dream baths and come-on eyelids,
yearning breaths and alphabetic poses –

Now a laid back T, now a sensuous S –
yet he doesn't creep up on me.
Instead I listen to the wind

Shaking memories from the trees.
But somewhere before morning,
unbeknown to me, he must have pounced,

As I was impregnated with a dream,
a gift from his prowling presence –
The one who makes no sound or leaves a footprint,

The thief who nightly steals your brain;
The-One-You-Don't-See-Coming –
my ancestors' other name for *Sleep*.

ACKNOWLEDGEMENTS

Acknowledgments are due to the following organisations and publications for first publication of some of these poems: 'In Search of Sleep', a response to the George Herbert's (1593-1633) poem 'Peace' (commissioned for Shakespeare's Globe Voice and Echo event, September 2015); 'Parallel World' commissioned for the anthology *Alice: Ekphrasis* (at the British Library), edited by Emer Gillespie, Abegail Morley and Catherine Smith (Joy Lane Publishing, 2016); 'Wherever They Lie' first appeared in *For Our Daughters* (website against violence to women initiated by Jean Calder); 'Night Muse' first appeared in *Hwaet! 20 Years of Ledbury Poetry Festival*, edited by Mark Fisher (Bloodaxe Books, 2016).

Thanks due to the following publications: *Acquainted with the Night: Excursions Through the World After Dark* by Christopher Dewdney (Bloomsbury, 2004); *Parabola* ('Sleep', vol. VII), which drew my attention to the folktale *The One You Don't See Coming* from *The Cow-Tail Switch*, edited by Harold Courlander and George Herzog (published by Square Fish, an imprint of Macmillan); as well the article, 'Time Out Of Time' by Paul Jordan-Smith; and special thanks to Stanley Greaves, Guyanese artist, whose painting 'Morning Mangoes' was used for the cover of this book.